Djibouti

Introduction

Welcome to the hidden jewel of the Horn of Africa, Djibouti. Nestled between Eritrea, Ethiopia, and Somalia, this small yet captivating nation is a true gem for travelers seeking unspoiled beauty, rich history, and a unique blend of cultures. Djibouti's diverse landscapes, from pristine beaches along the Red Sea to otherworldly deserts and rugged mountains, make it a destination like no other.

In this travel guide, we'll take you on a journey through Djibouti's natural wonders, historical sites, culinary delights, and local experiences. You'll discover the mesmerizing landscapes of Lake Assal, Ardoukoba Volcano, and the tranquil shores of Moucha Island. Dive into the heart of Djibouti's culture by exploring its vibrant markets, traditional villages, and historic sites, all of which reveal the deep-rooted heritage of the country.

Djibouti's culinary scene is a fusion of flavors influenced by Africa and the Middle East, with an emphasis on fresh seafood and vibrant spices. You'll have the chance to engage with the friendly locals, participate in cultural traditions, and experience life in this unique corner of the world.

While Djibouti may not be as well-traveled as some of its neighbors, its unspoiled beauty and tranquil ambiance are part of its allure. Whether you're a nature enthusiast, a history buff, or a traveler seeking an authentic coastal retreat, Djibouti offers an uncharted journey of discovery.

So, fasten your seatbelt and prepare to embark on an adventure that will take you from the depths of ancient history to the pristine shores of the Red Sea. Djibouti is waiting to share its secrets and captivating beauty with you. Welcome to the enchanting world of Djibouti.

Travel Essentials

Visa: Check the visa requirements for your nationality before traveling to Djibouti.

Language: French and Arabic are the official languages, but Afar and Somali are also widely spoken.

Currency: Djiboutian Franc (DJF)

Time Zone: East Africa Time (EAT) UTC+3

Weather: Djibouti has a hot, arid climate, so pack accordingly.

Top Places to Visit:

Lake Assal: This stunning saltwater lake is the lowest point in Africa and one of the saltiest bodies of water in the world. Its crystalline shores and the surrounding lunar-like landscape make for incredible photo opportunities.

Ardoukoba Volcano: For adventure seekers, this dormant volcano offers a challenging hike to its summit. You'll be rewarded with panoramic views and a glimpse into the geological wonders of the area.

Tadjoura: A coastal town known for its historical architecture, Tadjoura boasts colorful houses, mosques, and a lively market. Don't miss the chance to take a swim in the Red Sea or relax on the nearby beach.

Djibouti City: The capital is a bustling hub where you can explore lively markets, visit the Presidential Palace, and experience the fusion of African, Arabian, and French influences in its architecture and cuisine.

Moucha Island: A short boat ride from Djibouti City, Moucha Island offers pristine white-sand beaches, clear waters perfect for snorkeling, and a relaxed atmosphere.

Arta Plage: A coastal town with warm waters, Arta Plage is a popular spot for water sports like windsurfing, jet skiing, and swimming.

Day Forest National Park: Explore the lush greenery of Day Forest, home to various species of trees, birds, and wildlife. It's a tranquil escape from the arid landscapes of Djibouti.

Cultural Experiences:

Local Markets: Visit Djibouti's vibrant markets, like the Central Market in Djibouti City, to experience the local culture, buy traditional crafts, and sample delicious street food.

Hammams: Try a traditional hammam for a relaxing and cultural experience, similar to a Turkish bath.

Local Cuisine: Sample Djiboutian dishes like skoudehkaris (spiced rice and meat), sabayah (pancakes), and sambusa (samosas). Don't forget to sip on sweet Somali tea.

Cultural Festivals: Check local calendars for festivals like the Aïd-el-Fitr, which marks the end of Ramadan, and the National Day of Djibouti on June 27th.

Travel Tips:

Respect Local Customs: Djibouti is a conservative Muslim country, so dress modestly, especially when visiting mosques or rural areas.

Stay Hydrated: The climate is extremely hot and dry, so drink plenty of water to stay hydrated.

Health Precautions: Ensure your vaccinations are up to date and consult a healthcare professional for recommended vaccinations and medications.

Safety: Djibouti is generally safe for travelers, but exercise normal precautions and be aware of your surroundings.

Bargaining: Bargaining is common in local markets. Don't be afraid to haggle for a fair price.

Djibouti offers a unique blend of natural beauty, rich culture, and historical significance. Whether you're an adventurer or a cultural explorer, this African gem has something for everyone. Enjoy your journey through the captivating landscapes and warm hospitality of Djibouti!

Lake Assal

Lake Assal, located in Djibouti, is a unique natural wonder with a range of interesting features and attractions for visitors. Here are some of the things you can see and experience at Lake Assal:

Salt Flats: Lake Assal is renowned for its vast salt flats, which extend to the lake's shoreline. The dazzling white salt crusts make for a surreal and almost lunar landscape, perfect for photography.

Lowest Point in Africa: Lake Assal is the lowest point on the African continent and the third-lowest point on Earth. This natural depression lies about 509 feet (155 meters) below sea level, making it a geologically significant location.

Salt Pinnacles: As you explore the salt flats, you'll encounter unique salt formations known as salt pinnacles. These natural sculptures are created by the evaporation of the lake's water, leaving behind salt deposits.

Geothermal Springs: Near Lake Assal, you can find geothermal springs where hot water bubbles up from the Earth's interior. These springs provide a stark contrast to the otherwise harsh and arid surroundings.

Djibouti's Scenic Beauty: The surrounding landscapes, with the salt flats against the backdrop of the sea and the stark desert, create a breathtaking contrast. This area is a paradise for photographers and nature enthusiasts.

Wildlife: Although the area is quite harsh, you may spot some resilient wildlife, such as migratory birds, lizards, and insects. Keep an eye out for these unique adaptations to the extreme environment.

Adventure Activities: For those seeking adventure, you can take a guided hike to explore the salt flats and salt pinnacles. The unique landscapes offer an extraordinary experience for trekkers and nature lovers.

Local Culture: Lake Assal is not only a geological wonder but also holds cultural significance for the Afar people, one of Djibouti's indigenous communities. Engaging with local communities can provide insights into their way of life and traditions.

Scientific Interest: Lake Assal is of significant scientific interest due to its unique geological features. It has been studied by geologists and researchers to better understand the Earth's geology.

When visiting Lake Assal, remember to bring plenty of water, sunscreen, and appropriate clothing to protect yourself from the intense sun and heat. Exploring this extraordinary location is an opportunity to witness nature's wonders and experience the world from a different perspective.

foods from Lake Assal

Lake Assal in Djibouti is not particularly known for its cuisine, as it's primarily a geological and natural attraction. However, Djibouti, as a whole, offers a variety of dishes that reflect the rich culinary traditions of the region. While you may not find foods directly associated with Lake Assal, here are some of the best foods you can enjoy in Djibouti:

Skoudehkaris: This is Djibouti's national dish and is similar to pilaf. It's made with spiced rice, vegetables, and often meat (such as goat or chicken). The dish is known for its rich and aromatic flavors.

Lahoh: Lahoh is a type of spongy, sourdough pancake, similar to Ethiopian injera. It's a common accompaniment to many Djiboutian dishes and can be used to scoop up stews and sauces.

Sambusa: Sambusas are savory pastries filled with minced meat, vegetables, and sometimes lentils. They're a popular snack in Djibouti and can be found in local markets.

Iskudhexkaris: This is another popular rice dish in Djibouti. It's made with fragrant rice, vegetables, and meat, often flavored with a blend of spices.

Canjeero: Canjeero is a type of sourdough flatbread that is often served for breakfast. It's enjoyed with honey, butter, or a spicy meat stew.

Seafood: Given Djibouti's coastal location, you'll find an abundance of fresh seafood. Try dishes like grilled fish, lobster, and prawns prepared with local spices and flavors.

Spices and Sauces: Djiboutian cuisine is known for its use of spices like cumin, coriander, cardamom, and cloves. Harira, a spicy sauce, is commonly used to add flavor to dishes.

Sahel Coffee: Enjoy a cup of Sahel coffee, a strong and aromatic brew often flavored with spices like cinnamon and cardamom. It's a popular drink in Djibouti and a part of local culture.

Fresh Fruits: Djibouti's markets are filled with a variety of fresh fruits, including mangoes, bananas, papayas, and citrus fruits. These make for a refreshing and healthy snack.

When visiting Djibouti, you'll have the opportunity to savor a blend of flavors influenced by African, Middle Eastern, and French culinary traditions. Local restaurants and street vendors offer an array of dishes to choose from, making it a delightful culinary adventure for food enthusiasts. While Lake Assal may not have its own unique foods, the cuisine of Djibouti is sure to leave a lasting impression on your taste buds.

restaurants in Lake Assal

Lake Assal is a natural attraction known for its stunning salt flats and geological features, but it is not a location with restaurants or dining establishments. Lake Assal is situated in a remote, arid region in Djibouti, and visitors typically do not find restaurants or dining facilities directly at the lake.

To enjoy dining options, you would need to travel to nearby towns or cities, such as Tadjoura or Djibouti City. In these areas, you can find restaurants that offer Djiboutian and international cuisine. Here are a few popular restaurants in Djibouti City where you can savor local and international dishes:

La Chaumière: This restaurant offers a blend of French and Djiboutian cuisine in a charming atmosphere. It's known for its seafood dishes and has a great view of the sea.

Chez Abdo: A local favorite, Chez Abdo serves traditional Djiboutian dishes like skoudehkaris and grilled seafood. It's a casual and popular spot for both locals and tourists.

Moulouk Palace Restaurant: Located in Tadjoura, this restaurant offers an array of local and international dishes in a relaxed setting. It's particularly known for its fresh seafood.

L'Oasis Restaurant: This restaurant in Djibouti City specializes in Mediterranean cuisine and offers a variety of delicious dishes, including kebabs, shawarma, and fresh salads.

La Promenade des Thés: If you're looking for a place to enjoy tea, coffee, and pastries, this café in Djibouti City is a great choice. They serve a selection of beverages and light snacks.

While you won't find restaurants at Lake Assal itself, you can explore the local cuisine and dining options in nearby towns and cities. Djibouti offers a diverse culinary scene that combines African, Middle Eastern, and French influences, providing a range of flavors and experiences for food enthusiasts.

lesser known travel spots in Lake Assal

Lake Assal is primarily known for its stunning salt flats and its status as the lowest point in Africa. While there may not be many lesser-known travel spots directly within Lake Assal, the surrounding region of the Afar Triangle in Djibouti offers some unique and less-visited attractions for adventurous travelers. Here are a few lesser-known travel spots and activities in the Lake Assal region:

Afar Villages: The Afar people are indigenous to the region, and visiting their villages can provide valuable cultural insights. Engaging with local communities and learning about their traditional way of life can be a unique and enriching experience.

Geothermal Springs: The Lake Assal area is known for its geothermal activity. Explore the geothermal springs and witness bubbling hot water emerging from the Earth's surface. These springs are not as well-known as other geothermal destinations but are equally fascinating.

Soda Lakes: In addition to Lake Assal, there are other nearby soda lakes, such as Lake Abbe. These lakes have their own unique characteristics, including otherworldly landscapes and significant bird populations, making them ideal for birdwatching.

Hiking and Trekking: While the focus is often on Lake Assal, the surrounding landscapes are equally intriguing. Consider embarking on a trek or hike to explore the rugged terrain, rocky formations, and desert vistas. These areas are less frequented by tourists, providing a sense of solitude and adventure.

Rock Formations: The Afar region is known for its unusual and often surreal rock formations. Some of these formations resemble abstract sculptures, while others are the result of ancient volcanic activity. Exploring these unique geological wonders can be an otherworldly experience.

Salt Mining: Witness the traditional methods of salt extraction used by local Afar communities. This is an opportunity to gain insights into the labor-intensive process of harvesting salt from the lake.

Star Gazing: The remote location and lack of light pollution make the Lake Assal region an excellent spot for stargazing. On clear nights, you can enjoy breathtaking views of the night sky.

It's important to note that the Lake Assal region is remote and can be challenging to access. Travelers should be prepared for extreme heat, arid conditions, and limited facilities. Additionally, some areas may require permits, so it's advisable to check with local authorities or tour operators before embarking on these adventures. While these lesser-known spots may not be as developed as some more popular destinations, they offer a chance to experience the unspoiled beauty and cultural richness of the region.

activities in Lake Assal

Lake Assal is a unique natural wonder known for its salt flats and extreme geological features. While it's not a location with a wide range of activities like a typical tourist destination, there are some must-do experiences and activities you can enjoy when visiting Lake Assal:

Explore the Salt Flats: The vast salt flats surrounding Lake Assal are the main attraction. Take a walk on the salt crusts, observe the intricate salt formations, and appreciate the surreal, almost lunar-like landscape.

Take Photographs: Lake Assal offers unparalleled opportunities for photography. Capture the stark contrast of the white salt flats against the blue waters of the lake and the surrounding arid desert.

Geothermal Springs: Visit the nearby geothermal springs, where hot water bubbles up from the Earth's interior. It's a unique experience to witness these natural phenomena in the otherwise harsh environment.

Hiking and Trekking: While not necessarily known for hiking, you can explore the region on foot, especially the rugged terrain surrounding the lake. Make sure to be prepared with proper footwear, water, and sun protection.

Birdwatching: Lake Assal and the surrounding area are home to various bird species. Bring binoculars and enjoy birdwatching, especially around nearby soda lakes and saltwater marshes.

Cultural Interactions: Engage with the local Afar communities and learn about their traditional way of life. The Afar people have adapted to the challenging environment and have a rich cultural heritage.

Salt Mining Observation: Witness the traditional methods of salt extraction used by local Afar communities. This labor-intensive process involves harvesting salt from the lake, which has been a way of life for generations.

Stargazing: The remote location of Lake Assal offers exceptional stargazing opportunities. On clear nights, you can admire the beauty of the night sky without the interference of light pollution.

Study Geology: If you have an interest in geology, Lake Assal is a fascinating place to explore. The geological features and unique salt formations make it a natural classroom for those interested in the Earth's processes.

Enjoy a Picnic: While there may not be restaurants at Lake Assal, you can bring your own picnic and enjoy a meal in this extraordinary setting. Be sure to carry enough water and snacks.

Please be aware that the climate around Lake Assal is extremely hot and arid, and there may be limited facilities. Ensure you are well-prepared with essentials like water, sunscreen, appropriate clothing, and any necessary permits if you plan to explore the region. Always respect the local environment and culture while enjoying your experiences at Lake Assal.

nightlife in Lake Assal

Lake Assal is a natural attraction known for its salt flats and geological features, but it is not a location with a nightlife scene. In fact, the Lake Assal region is remote and sparsely populated, primarily visited for its natural beauty and geological significance. As a result, you won't find nightlife spots, bars, or entertainment venues in the immediate vicinity of Lake Assal.

If you are looking for nightlife and entertainment options, you would need to travel to nearby towns and cities, such as Djibouti City. Djibouti City has a modest nightlife scene, with some restaurants, cafes, and hotels offering evening entertainment. You can find a mix of traditional Djiboutian music and dance performances, as well as a limited selection of bars and clubs.

Keep in mind that Djibouti, as a whole, is a conservative Muslim country, and the nightlife scene is not as vibrant or extensive as in many other destinations. Alcohol consumption may be limited, and venues that serve alcohol are relatively few.

While you won't experience nightlife in the Lake Assal region itself, you can enjoy the tranquil and serene atmosphere of the natural surroundings. Visitors often come to Lake Assal to unwind and appreciate the breathtaking landscapes and unique geological features rather than seeking active nightlife experiences.

hotels in Lake Assal

As of my last knowledge update in September 2021, Lake Assal is a natural attraction located in a remote, arid region in Djibouti. It is not an area known for hotels or accommodations. Travelers interested in visiting Lake Assal typically stay in nearby towns or cities, such as Tadjoura or Djibouti City, and then make a day trip to Lake Assal. Here are some recommended hotels in Djibouti City and Tadjoura:

Djibouti City:

Sheraton Djibouti Hotel: This international chain hotel offers modern amenities and a convenient location on the shores of the Red Sea. It has comfortable rooms and a range of facilities, including restaurants and a swimming pool.

Djibouti Palace Kempinski: Another luxury option in Djibouti City, this hotel provides elegant accommodations, restaurants, a spa, and beautiful sea views.

Djibouti Arta Youth Hostel: A more budget-friendly option, this hostel offers dormitory-style accommodations and is suitable for backpackers and travelers on a budget.

Auberge le Héron: This cozy and charming boutique hotel is located near the seafront and offers comfortable rooms and a restaurant serving both local and international dishes.

Tadjoura:

Auberge Le Mirage: This small hotel in Tadjoura offers simple but comfortable accommodations. It's an ideal base for exploring the town and the nearby attractions.

La Siesta Hotel: Another option in Tadjoura, La Siesta Hotel provides basic yet clean and comfortable rooms. It's known for its friendly staff and affordability.

Please note that the availability and quality of accommodations may vary, and it's advisable to check the latest information and reviews from travel websites or contact hotels directly for the most up-to-date information and availability.

Keep in mind that the Lake Assal region is remote and does not have hotels directly at the lake. Travelers often make day trips to Lake Assal from nearby towns and cities, and accommodations are more readily available in these areas. Additionally, the hotel scene in Djibouti may have evolved since my last update, so it's a good idea to research the latest options and reviews for the most current information.

Ardoukoba Volcano

Ardoukoba Volcano, located in Djibouti, is a dormant volcano and a fascinating natural attraction for adventurous travelers. Here are some of the things you can see and experience when visiting Ardoukoba Volcano:

Volcanic Landscape: Ardoukoba Volcano offers a unique opportunity to explore a volcanic landscape. The rocky terrain, lava formations, and the volcano's distinct shape are a captivating sight.

Hiking: One of the main activities at Ardoukoba is hiking. The volcano is relatively easy to climb, and the hike takes you to its summit, which provides spectacular panoramic views of the surrounding area, including Lake Assal and the Red Sea.

Crater: At the top of Ardoukoba, you can explore the volcanic crater. The view inside the crater reveals the geological history of the volcano and the lava flows.

Flora and Fauna: While the terrain is harsh and arid, you can still find some resilient plant life that has adapted to the conditions. Keep an eye out for unique desert flora, and you might spot birds and insects.

Geological Features: The volcano itself and the surrounding area showcase various geological features, making it an interesting destination for geology enthusiasts. You can observe different types of rocks, mineral deposits, and lava formations.

Photography: Ardoukoba's unique landscape, with its dramatic views, makes it an excellent location for photography. Be sure to capture the otherworldly scenery and the contrasting colors and textures.

Volcanic History: Learn about the volcanic history of Ardoukoba and the region. The volcano's eruptions and geological significance can be of interest to those interested in earth sciences.

Adventure: Climbing a volcano is an adventure in itself. Enjoy the thrill of reaching the summit and taking in the breathtaking vistas. Be sure to come prepared with proper hiking gear and plenty of water.

Afar Culture: The Afar people, who inhabit the region, have a rich culture that has adapted to the volcanic landscape. Engaging with the local Afar communities can provide insights into their way of life and traditions.

Visiting Ardoukoba Volcano is an opportunity to experience the geological wonders of Djibouti and take in some of the most dramatic landscapes in the country. It's essential to be well-prepared for the hike and the arid climate, ensuring you have the necessary equipment and supplies for a safe and enjoyable experience.

foods from Ardoukoba Volcano

Ardoukoba Volcano is a geological attraction located in a remote and arid region of Djibouti. It is not an area known for its cuisine or culinary offerings. In fact, the immediate vicinity of Ardoukoba Volcano does not have restaurants or dining establishments. Travelers typically make day trips to the volcano from nearby towns and cities like Djibouti City or Tadjoura for hiking and geological exploration.

If you are looking for food while visiting Ardoukoba, it's advisable to bring your own provisions or snacks, as there are no restaurants or food vendors in the immediate area. Be sure to carry ample water and any necessary supplies for your hike and exploration of the volcano.

In the towns and cities near Ardoukoba, such as Djibouti City or Tadjoura, you can enjoy a variety of Djiboutian dishes, including skoudehkaris (spiced rice and meat), sambusa (samosas), and fresh seafood, given their coastal locations. Djibouti cuisine is influenced by a blend of African, Middle Eastern, and French culinary traditions, offering a mix of flavors and dishes for travelers to explore.

While you may not find specific foods associated with Ardoukoba Volcano, the culinary experiences in Djibouti's towns and cities can provide a delicious and culturally rich part of your visit.

restaurants in Ardoukoba Volcano

Ardoukoba Volcano is a geological attraction located in a remote and arid region in Djibouti. It is not an area with restaurants or dining establishments. Visitors typically make day trips to the volcano from nearby towns and cities such as Djibouti City or Tadjoura for hiking and geological exploration.

The immediate vicinity of Ardoukoba Volcano does not offer dining options, and there are no restaurants or food vendors in the area. Travelers are often advised to bring their own provisions, including water and snacks, when visiting the volcano.

If you are looking for dining options, you will need to travel to nearby towns and cities like Djibouti City or Tadjoura. These places have restaurants where you can enjoy Djiboutian and international cuisine. Djibouti City, in particular, offers a range of dining options, from local dishes to international fare.

While Ardoukoba Volcano is not a location for dining, the surrounding regions provide opportunities to savor Djibouti's unique culinary culture, which combines African, Middle Eastern, and French influences, offering a diverse range of flavors and dishes to explore.

lesser known travel spots in Ardoukoba Volcano

Ardoukoba Volcano is a geological attraction located in a remote and arid region of Djibouti. While the volcano itself is the primary point of interest, there are several lesser-known travel spots and attractions in the surrounding area that can add depth to your visit:

Salt Flats and Geothermal Springs: The region around Ardoukoba Volcano features salt flats and geothermal springs. These areas offer unique geological formations and the chance to observe the geothermal activity of the region.

Afar Villages: The Afar people, who inhabit the region, have adapted to the challenging environment. Visiting Afar villages provides insights into their way of life and cultural traditions. Engaging with local communities can be an enriching cultural experience.

Hiking and Exploration: While the volcano itself is a popular hiking destination, the surrounding rugged terrain and rocky landscapes offer opportunities for trekking and geological exploration. These areas are less frequented by tourists, providing a sense of solitude and adventure.

Desert Flora and Fauna: Despite the arid conditions, you can find unique plant and animal life that has adapted to the environment. Keep an eye out for resilient desert flora and the possibility of spotting bird and insect species.

Rock Formations: The Ardoukoba region is known for unusual rock formations. Some of these formations resemble abstract sculptures, while others are the result of ancient volcanic activity. Exploring these geological wonders can be a fascinating experience.

Cultural Interactions: Engaging with the local Afar communities is an opportunity to learn about their traditional way of life, cultural practices, and the challenges of living in this remote region.

Stargazing: The remote location of Ardoukoba Volcano offers exceptional stargazing opportunities. On clear nights, you can enjoy breathtaking views of the night sky without the interference of light pollution.

While the Ardoukoba Volcano itself is the primary attraction, these lesser-known travel spots and activities in the surrounding region allow you to delve deeper into the natural beauty and cultural richness of the area. Be sure to prepare adequately for the challenging and remote environment, including bringing essentials like water, sunscreen, and proper hiking gear. Additionally, some areas may require permits or local guidance, so it's a good idea to check with authorities or tour operators before exploring these lesser-known spots.

activities in Ardoukoba Volcano

Ardoukoba Volcano, located in Djibouti, offers a unique and adventurous experience for travelers interested in geology and natural landscapes. Here are some activities you can enjoy when visiting Ardoukoba Volcano:

Hiking and Trekking: The most popular activity at Ardoukoba is hiking. You can embark on a hike to the summit of the volcano, which provides spectacular panoramic views of the surrounding area, including Lake Assal and the Red Sea. The hike is relatively moderate in difficulty and is an excellent way to explore the volcanic terrain.

Explore the Crater: At the top of Ardoukoba Volcano, you can venture into the volcanic crater itself. This provides an opportunity to examine the geological history of the volcano and the lava formations within.

Photography: Ardoukoba's unique and dramatic landscape, with its contrasting colors and textures, makes it an excellent location for photography. Be sure to capture the otherworldly scenery and the vistas from the summit.

Geological Exploration: The volcano and its surroundings offer various geological features and formations. Geology enthusiasts can examine different types of rocks, mineral deposits, and lava flows to gain a deeper understanding of the region's geological history.

Birdwatching: The Ardoukoba region, with its varying terrain, may attract bird species. Birdwatchers can enjoy spotting various avian species, so be sure to bring binoculars and a field guide if you have an interest in ornithology.

Flora and Fauna Observation: While the environment is harsh and arid, you can still find resilient plant life and the possibility of spotting desert wildlife and insects. Explore the local flora and fauna to gain insights into how life adapts to this challenging landscape.

Stargazing: The remote location of Ardoukoba Volcano provides excellent conditions for stargazing. On clear nights, you can appreciate the beauty of the night sky without the interference of light pollution.

Cultural Interaction: While Ardoukoba Volcano itself may not have cultural sites, you can engage with the local Afar communities in the region. Learning about their traditional way of life and cultural practices can provide valuable insights into the local culture and customs.

Before embarking on your visit to Ardoukoba Volcano, ensure you are well-prepared for the arid and challenging environment. It's essential to have proper hiking gear, adequate water, and sun protection to ensure a safe and enjoyable experience. Always respect the natural surroundings and any local guidelines or restrictions to help preserve the unique geological features of the area.

nightlife in Ardoukoba Volcano

Ardoukoba Volcano is a geological attraction located in a remote and arid region of Djibouti. It is not an area with nightlife or entertainment options. Visitors come to Ardoukoba for its natural beauty, geological features, and outdoor activities, not for nightlife or social activities.

The immediate vicinity of Ardoukoba Volcano does not offer any nightlife spots, bars, or entertainment venues. The focus of a visit to Ardoukoba is on daytime activities like hiking, exploring the volcano, and enjoying the natural landscapes.

If you are interested in nightlife, you would need to travel to nearby towns and cities, such as Djibouti City or Tadjoura, where you can find a limited nightlife scene. Djibouti City has a few restaurants, cafes, and hotels that offer evening entertainment, including traditional Djiboutian music and dance performances, as well as a limited selection of bars and clubs.

It's important to note that Djibouti, as a whole, is a conservative Muslim country, and the nightlife scene is not as vibrant or extensive as in many other tourist destinations. Alcohol consumption may be limited, and venues that serve alcohol are relatively few.

While Ardoukoba Volcano itself does not offer nightlife experiences, it provides a tranquil and serene environment where visitors can immerse themselves in the beauty of the natural surroundings and enjoy outdoor activities during the day.

hotels in Ardoukoba Volcano

Ardoukoba Volcano is located in a remote and arid region of Djibouti and is not known for its accommodations or hotels. Travelers typically make day trips to Ardoukoba from nearby towns or cities, such as Djibouti City or Tadjoura, and return to those locations for lodging.

In Djibouti City and Tadjoura, you can find a range of accommodations, including hotels and guesthouses. Here are some recommended options in these towns:

Djibouti City:

Sheraton Djibouti Hotel: An international chain hotel with modern amenities, comfortable rooms, and beautiful sea views. It offers a range of facilities, including restaurants, a swimming pool, and a fitness center.

Djibouti Palace Kempinski: A luxury hotel in Djibouti City, offering elegant accommodations, multiple dining options, a spa, and sea-facing rooms.

La Siesta Hotel: A more budget-friendly option with clean and comfortable rooms, situated near the seafront. It's known for its affordability and friendly staff.

Tadjoura:

Auberge Le Mirage: This small hotel in Tadjoura offers simple but comfortable accommodations. It's an ideal base for exploring the town and the nearby attractions.

La Siesta Hotel Tadjoura: An extension of the La Siesta Hotel in Djibouti City, this property provides basic yet clean and comfortable rooms in Tadjoura.

Please note that the availability and quality of accommodations may vary, and it's advisable to check the latest information and reviews from travel websites or contact hotels directly for the most up-to-date information and availability.

Keep in mind that the Lake Assal region is remote, and visitors often make day trips to Ardoukoba Volcano from nearby towns and cities. The hotel scene in Djibouti may have evolved since my last update, so it's a good idea to research the latest options and reviews for the most current information.

Tadjoura

Tadjoura is a charming coastal town in Djibouti, known for its relaxed atmosphere and beautiful surroundings. While it's not a bustling tourist destination, Tadjoura offers a range of interesting sights and attractions for travelers who appreciate culture, history, and natural beauty. Here are some of the things you can see and do in Tadjoura:

Tadjoura Beach: The town boasts a picturesque beach with soft white sand and clear blue waters. It's a lovely spot for swimming, sunbathing, and relaxing by the sea.

Tadjoura Mosque: The town's central mosque, also known as the Tadjoura Grand Mosque, is a historic site with a distinctive architecture that combines Islamic and local design elements. Visitors can admire its unique features.

Port of Tadjoura: Take a stroll along the picturesque port area, which is lined with fishing boats and offers a glimpse into the town's maritime activities. It's a pleasant place for a leisurely walk.

Tadjoura Market: Visit the local market to experience the daily life and culture of the town's residents. You can find various goods, including fresh produce, spices, textiles, and handicrafts.

Dolphins at Ras Ali: About 25 kilometers from Tadjoura, you can visit Ras Ali, a cape that is home to a resident population of dolphins. Boat tours are available for dolphin watching.

Lac Assal (Lake Assal): While Lake Assal is not in Tadjoura, it's a popular day trip destination from the town. The lake is known for its immense salt flats and unique geological features.

Hot Springs: Near Tadjoura, you can explore geothermal springs, which are part of the region's unique geological landscape.

Desert Landscapes: Tadjoura is surrounded by desert terrain and rocky landscapes, making it an ideal location for those interested in desert hiking and exploration.

Cultural Encounters: Engage with the local Afar communities and learn about their traditional way of life and cultural practices. The people of Tadjoura are known for their rich cultural heritage.

Tadjoura is a place to unwind, enjoy the coastal scenery, and immerse yourself in local culture. It provides a more relaxed and authentic experience compared to the busier cities like Djibouti City. When visiting Tadjoura, be mindful of local customs and traditions, and respect the environment and culture of the region.

foods from Tadjoura

Tadjoura, like the rest of Djibouti, offers a culinary scene influenced by various cultures, including African, Middle Eastern, and French flavors. While it may not have as wide a variety of dining options as more urban centers, there are still some delicious dishes to savor in Tadjoura. Here are some of the best foods you can enjoy in the area:

Skoudehkaris: Skoudehkaris is Djibouti's national dish, and you can find it in Tadjoura. It's a flavorful rice dish made with spices, vegetables, and meat, often served with yogurt or a tomato sauce.

Lahoh: Lahoh is a type of spongy, sourdough pancake similar to Ethiopian injera. It's commonly served in Tadjoura and is used to scoop up stews and sauces.

Sambusa: Sambusas are savory pastries filled with minced meat, vegetables, and sometimes lentils. They're a popular snack and appetizer in Djibouti.

Grilled Seafood: Given Tadjoura's coastal location, you can enjoy an array of fresh seafood, including fish, lobster, prawns, and octopus. These are often grilled and seasoned with local spices.

Canjeero: Canjeero is a type of sourdough flatbread that is often served for breakfast or as a side dish. It's enjoyed with honey, butter, or a spicy meat stew.

Fresh Fruits: Tadjoura's markets are filled with a variety of fresh fruits, including mangoes, bananas, papayas, and citrus fruits. These make for a refreshing and healthy snack.

Tea and Coffee: Enjoy traditional Djiboutian tea or coffee, often flavored with spices like cardamom and served with small, sweet pastries.

While Tadjoura may not have the extensive dining scene found in larger cities, the local cuisine reflects the rich cultural diversity of Djibouti. Exploring the local dishes in Tadjoura is an opportunity to experience the flavors and culinary traditions of this unique region. Be sure to visit local eateries and engage with the friendly residents to get the most authentic dining experience.

restaurants in Tadjoura

Tadjoura is a picturesque coastal town in Djibouti known for its natural beauty and cultural charm. While it may not have a bustling restaurant scene like more prominent cities, you can still find local eateries and restaurants that offer traditional Djiboutian dishes. Here are a few dining spots in Tadjoura where you can enjoy local cuisine:

Tadjoura Restaurant: This restaurant is a great place to sample traditional Djiboutian dishes. You can expect to find skoudehkaris (spiced rice with meat), grilled seafood, and other local specialties.

Local Eateries: Tadjoura has various small local eateries and food stalls where you can enjoy homemade, authentic Djiboutian dishes. These places offer a casual and affordable dining experience.

Tadjoura Café: Visit a local café in Tadjoura for a cup of Djiboutian tea or coffee, often served with small pastries. It's a relaxing spot to enjoy a warm beverage and soak in the local atmosphere.

Market Food: Tadjoura's market is a place to try freshly prepared snacks and dishes. Vendors may offer sambusas, canjeero, and other local delicacies.

While the restaurant scene in Tadjoura may not be as extensive as in larger cities, the local eateries provide a chance to savor authentic Djiboutian cuisine and engage with the friendly residents. It's also worth exploring the fresh seafood options in the area, as Tadjoura's coastal location ensures a supply of delicious seafood dishes. When dining in Tadjoura, you can experience the flavors and culinary traditions of this charming coastal town.

lesser known travel spots in Tadjoura

Tadjoura is a quieter and less touristy destination in Djibouti, but it offers a tranquil and culturally rich experience. While it may not have numerous well-known tourist spots, there are some lesser-known attractions and activities in and around Tadjoura that you can explore:

Tadjoura Island: Located in the Gulf of Tadjoura, this island offers beautiful beaches, crystal-clear waters, and opportunities for snorkeling and swimming. It's a serene and lesser-visited spot for relaxation.

Moucha Island: Similar to Tadjoura Island, Moucha Island is known for its beautiful beaches, coral reefs, and underwater marine life. It's a great place for water activities such as snorkeling and scuba diving.

Afar Villages: Surrounding Tadjoura are Afar villages that provide insights into the traditional way of life of the Afar people. You can engage with the locals and learn about their customs and traditions.

Cave of Mousa Ali: Located about an hour's drive from Tadjoura, this cave is considered a holy site by the local Afar population. It's a fascinating place for those interested in the religious and cultural significance of the region.

Hot Springs: There are hot springs near Tadjoura that are part of the region's unique geothermal landscape. These springs are not as well-known as some other geothermal spots in Djibouti.

Hiking and Exploring Nature: The rugged terrain around Tadjoura offers opportunities for hiking and exploring. You can venture into the nearby hills and desert landscapes.

Fishing: Engage in traditional fishing with local fishermen, which is a common activity in Tadjoura due to its coastal location.

Dhow Tours: You can take a traditional dhow boat tour along the coast to explore the beautiful shoreline and nearby islands.

Cultural Interactions: Interact with the local Afar communities to learn about their way of life and experience their hospitality and culture.

While Tadjoura may not have the same level of tourist infrastructure as more developed destinations, its natural beauty, cultural richness, and the opportunity to connect with local communities make it a unique and lesser-visited travel spot in Djibouti. Travelers looking for an authentic and tranquil experience will find Tadjoura to be a hidden gem. Be sure to plan and prepare adequately for your visit, especially when venturing into more remote areas.

activities in Tadjoura

Tadjoura, a charming coastal town in Djibouti, offers a serene and culturally rich atmosphere, making it an ideal destination for travelers looking for a relaxed and authentic experience. While Tadjoura may not have the bustling tourist activities found in larger cities, it offers several activities that provide insight into the local culture and natural beauty. Here are some activities you should experience when visiting Tadjoura:

Beach Relaxation: Enjoy the beautiful beaches of Tadjoura. The soft white sands and clear waters make it a perfect spot for swimming, sunbathing, and relaxing by the sea.

Tadjoura Mosque: Visit the town's central mosque, Tadjoura Grand Mosque, and appreciate its unique architecture, which blends Islamic and local design elements.

Tadjoura Market: Explore the local market to witness daily life and culture in Tadjoura. You can find a variety of goods, including fresh produce, spices, textiles, and handicrafts.

Seafood Dining: Savor the delicious seafood in Tadjoura. Given its coastal location, you can enjoy fresh fish, lobster, prawns, and octopus, often grilled and seasoned with local spices.

Cultural Interaction: Engage with the local Afar communities and learn about their traditional way of life, cultural practices, and customs. The Afar people have a rich cultural heritage, and getting to know them is an enriching experience.

Boat Tours: Consider taking a boat tour along the coast to explore the picturesque shoreline and visit nearby islands, such as Tadjoura Island or Moucha Island.

Cave of Mousa Ali: Explore the Cave of Mousa Ali, a significant religious site for the local Afar population. The cave is known for its unique geological features and cultural importance.

Water Activities: Enjoy snorkeling and swimming in the clear waters of the nearby islands. You can also try traditional fishing with local fishermen.

Hiking and Desert Exploration: Venture into the surrounding desert landscapes for hiking and exploring. The rocky terrains offer opportunities for those interested in outdoor activities.

Local Cuisine: Taste traditional Djiboutian dishes, such as skoudehkaris (spiced rice and meat) and sambusa (samosas), in local eateries and market stalls.

Dolphin Watching: If you visit Ras Ali, about 25 kilometers from Tadjoura, you can take boat tours for dolphin watching.

Tadjoura is a place to unwind, soak in the local culture, and immerse yourself in the coastal beauty of Djibouti. Be respectful of local customs and traditions, and enjoy the tranquil and authentic atmosphere of this charming coastal town.

nightlife in Tadjoura

Tadjoura is a peaceful coastal town in Djibouti, known for its relaxed atmosphere and cultural charm. While it offers a serene and authentic travel experience, it is not a destination with a vibrant nightlife scene. The town tends to be quiet in the evenings, and you won't find a range of nightlife spots, bars, or entertainment venues as you might in larger cities.

Tadjoura's nightlife is primarily centered around quiet and laid-back activities. Evenings are an excellent time to unwind and enjoy the tranquil coastal ambiance. You can take leisurely walks by the beach, relax at local cafes, or engage in quiet conversations with the friendly residents.

If you're looking for a more vibrant nightlife scene with bars, clubs, and live entertainment, you would need to consider traveling to larger cities in Djibouti, such as Djibouti City. Djibouti City offers a limited nightlife scene with a few restaurants, cafes, and hotels that offer evening entertainment, including traditional Djiboutian music and dance performances. Keep in mind that Djibouti, as a whole, is a conservative Muslim country, and the nightlife scene is not as extensive as in many other destinations.

Tadjoura, with its coastal beauty and cultural richness, is better suited for travelers seeking a peaceful and authentic experience, enjoying the natural beauty and engaging with local communities. While you may not find active nightlife in Tadjoura, the town provides a unique and serene environment for travelers who appreciate a more relaxed and cultural travel experience.

hotels in Tadjoura

Tadjoura is a tranquil coastal town in Djibouti, and while it may not have the extensive hotel options found in larger cities, there are a few places where you can find accommodation. Here are a couple of the options you might consider when looking for the best hotels in Tadjoura:

Auberge Le Mirage: This is a small and charming hotel in Tadjoura. It offers simple yet comfortable accommodations and a friendly atmosphere. The hotel is known for its picturesque views and is an excellent base for exploring the town and the surrounding area.

La Siesta Hotel Tadjoura: La Siesta Hotel in Tadjoura offers clean and comfortable rooms. It is an extension of the La Siesta Hotel in Djibouti City, which is known for its affordability and friendly staff.

Please keep in mind that Tadjoura is a quieter and less touristy destination, and the hotel scene is limited in comparison to larger cities like Djibouti City. Accommodations in Tadjoura are generally simpler, and the emphasis is on the natural beauty, cultural experiences, and the relaxed coastal atmosphere of the town.

It's advisable to check the latest information and reviews from travel websites or contact the hotels directly for the most up-to-date information and availability, as the hotel scene may have evolved since my last knowledge update in September 2021.

Djibouti City

Djibouti City, the capital of Djibouti, is a diverse and vibrant urban center with a mix of cultures, history, and modern amenities. It serves as the country's political, economic, and cultural hub. Here are some of the attractions and things you can see in Djibouti City:

Haramous Market: A bustling and colorful market where you can explore local goods, from spices and fresh produce to textiles and artisan crafts. It offers a taste of the city's daily life.

Le Marché Central: Another lively market where you can shop for a wide range of products, including local handicrafts, clothing, and jewelry.

Djibouti Palace Kempinski: This luxurious hotel on the shores of the Red Sea is known for its grandeur, international dining options, and beautiful sea views.

Presidential Palace: Though not open to the public, you can admire the exterior of the Presidential Palace, an architectural landmark with a distinctive design.

Avenue 26th June: This bustling street in Djibouti City is home to various shops, cafes, and restaurants, offering a taste of the city's modern lifestyle.

Central Mosque: Djibouti City's central mosque is an iconic religious site with impressive architecture and a central location in the city.

Place Menelik: A public square and gathering place where you can experience local culture, especially during festivals and events.

French Cultural Center: A hub for cultural events, exhibitions, and language courses, offering insight into the French influence on Djibouti.

Port of Djibouti: Djibouti City is a major transportation hub, and the port is one of the busiest in the region. You can observe the comings and goings of ships, adding to the city's cosmopolitan feel.

Djibouti-Ambouli International Airport: While it may seem unusual, the airport itself can be an attraction due to its unique design and the incredible view of the city and the surrounding landscapes.

Lake Assal: Although not in the city, Lake Assal is a must-see natural wonder and a popular day trip destination from Djibouti City. It is known for its immense salt flats and unique geological features.

Day Excursions: Djibouti City serves as a starting point for various day trips to explore the diverse landscapes of Djibouti, including Ardoukoba Volcano, the Goda Mountains, and the salt flats.

Djibouti City offers a blend of modern urban life, historical sites, and opportunities to immerse yourself in the local culture. You can experience a mix of French and East African influences in this cosmopolitan city. Be sure to explore the markets, savor the local cuisine, and enjoy the natural beauty of the surrounding landscapes during your visit.

foods from Djibouti City

Djibouti City offers a diverse culinary scene influenced by African, Middle Eastern, and French flavors. The local cuisine combines unique ingredients and traditional dishes that reflect the country's cultural diversity. Here are some of the best foods you can savor in Djibouti City:

Skoudehkaris: Djibouti's national dish, skoudehkaris, is a flavorful rice dish made with spices, vegetables, and meat (typically goat, camel, or lamb). It's often served with a tomato-based sauce or yogurt.

Sambusa: Sambusas are savory pastries filled with minced meat, vegetables, and sometimes lentils. They are a popular snack and appetizer in Djibouti City.

Canjeero: Canjeero is a sourdough flatbread similar to Ethiopian injera. It is often served for breakfast or as a side dish and is used to scoop up stews and sauces.

Lahoh: Lahoh is a spongy, sourdough pancake that is also a common breakfast item, enjoyed with honey, butter, or spicy meat stews.

Biryanis and Stews: You'll find a variety of aromatic biryani rice dishes, as well as hearty meat and vegetable stews, in Djibouti City.

Seafood: Djibouti's coastal location ensures a plentiful supply of fresh seafood, including fish, lobster, prawns, and octopus. These are often grilled and seasoned with local spices.

Injera: Injera, a sourdough flatbread, is a common accompaniment to many dishes in Djibouti City, and it's especially popular among the Afar people.

Café Djibouti: Try traditional Djiboutian tea or coffee, often flavored with spices like cardamom and served with small pastries or snacks in local cafes.

Djiboutian Spices: Djibouti is known for its unique blend of spices, such as hawayej, which is used to season many dishes and adds depth of flavor to the cuisine.

Fruits: Enjoy fresh fruits, such as mangoes, bananas, papayas, and citrus fruits, which are often sold in local markets.

Exploring the local cuisine of Djibouti City is a delightful way to experience the country's rich cultural heritage and enjoy a blend of flavors from East Africa, the Middle East, and France. Be sure to visit local eateries, markets, and restaurants to savor the diverse culinary offerings of this vibrant city.

restaurants in Djibouti City

Djibouti City offers a variety of dining options that showcase the country's diverse culinary traditions, influenced by African, Middle Eastern, and French flavors. While the restaurant scene may not be as extensive as in larger cities, there are several places where you can enjoy delicious food and local specialties. Here are some of the best restaurants in Djibouti City:

Ali Baba Restaurant: Known for its Middle Eastern cuisine, Ali Baba offers a selection of shawarma, kebabs, and falafel. The restaurant provides an authentic taste of Middle Eastern flavors in Djibouti City.

Bab El Mandeb Restaurant: This restaurant serves a mix of international and local dishes, making it a great place to sample Djiboutian cuisine as well as enjoy a variety of other options.

La Place Restaurant: Located at Djibouti's Kempinski Hotel, La Place offers a sophisticated dining experience. It specializes in international cuisine and seafood, with beautiful views of the Red Sea.

Taj Mahal Restaurant: For lovers of Indian cuisine, Taj Mahal provides an array of flavorful Indian dishes, including biryanis, curries, and tandoori specialties.

Tandoor Restaurant: Another excellent choice for Indian cuisine, Tandoor is known for its richly spiced dishes and a cozy, welcoming atmosphere.

Le Yémen Restaurant: This restaurant offers a taste of Yemeni cuisine, with dishes like mandi (slow-cooked meat and rice) and foul (spiced fava beans).

Le Bâteau Pirate: Located on a boat in the harbor, this unique dining spot serves seafood and a variety of international dishes, offering a memorable setting for a meal.

Kulub Restaurant: A popular spot for traditional Djiboutian food, Kulub serves local specialties like skoudehkaris and sambusas.

Saaha Restaurant: Situated in the Sheraton Djibouti Hotel, Saaha offers an array of international cuisine in a luxurious setting with beautiful sea views.

Le Pêcheur Restaurant: Known for its seafood, this restaurant serves a range of fresh catches, such as grilled fish, prawns, and lobster.

Please note that the restaurant scene in Djibouti City may have evolved since my last update in September 2021. It's a good idea to check the latest information, reviews, and recommendations from travel websites or locals for the most current dining options and experiences. Djibouti City's dining scene caters to a variety of tastes, and you can enjoy the fusion of different culinary traditions in this cosmopolitan city.

lesser known travel spots in Djibouti City

Djibouti City, although a small capital, has some lesser-known travel spots and attractions that offer unique insights into the culture, history, and natural beauty of Djibouti. While these may not be as famous as some of the more popular tourist destinations, they provide a distinct and authentic travel experience. Here are some lesser-known travel spots in Djibouti City:

Arta Plage: Located on the outskirts of Djibouti City, Arta Plage is a quiet and serene beach area. It's an ideal spot for relaxation and enjoying the Red Sea's tranquil waters.

Horseback Riding in the Goda Mountains: Explore the scenic landscapes and local villages in the Goda Mountains on horseback. This unique experience allows you to connect with the natural beauty of the region.

Guedi Plateau: The Guedi Plateau is a volcanic plateau with unique geological features, including lava formations. It's a less-visited site that offers fascinating landscapes and the opportunity for geological exploration.

Hamoudi Mosque: While it's not as well-known as the Central Mosque in Djibouti City, the Hamoudi Mosque has beautiful architecture and a peaceful atmosphere. It's a place to admire Islamic design.

Hiking and Trekking in the Goda Mountains: The Goda Mountains offer hiking and trekking opportunities that are less crowded than more popular sites. The trails lead through unique landscapes and offer fantastic views.

The Day Forest National Park: Located near Djibouti City, this national park provides an opportunity to observe Djibouti's flora and fauna, including native birds and wildlife. It's a peaceful natural retreat.

Cultural Experiences: Seek out opportunities to engage with local communities, attend traditional ceremonies, and learn about the customs and way of life of Djiboutian people. These cultural interactions can provide a deeper understanding of the local culture.

Djiboutian Spices Market: Explore local markets to discover Djibouti's unique spices, like hawayej, which are used to flavor many traditional dishes. You can also find herbs and spices with medicinal properties.

While Djibouti City itself is not known for its tourist attractions, these lesser-known travel spots offer a chance to immerse yourself in the local culture, appreciate the natural beauty of the region, and discover hidden gems in this charming East African city. Be sure to inquire locally for any restrictions, permits, or guided tours that may be necessary to access some of these spots.

activities in Djibouti City

Djibouti City, the capital of Djibouti, offers a range of activities that allow you to immerse yourself in the local culture, explore the history, and enjoy the natural beauty of the region. Here are some activities you must experience while in Djibouti City:

Visit the Markets: Explore Djibouti City's vibrant markets, such as the Haramous Market and Le Marché Central. These are great places to experience local life, shop for spices, fresh produce, textiles, and crafts, and interact with friendly vendors.

Sample Djiboutian Cuisine: Savor the flavors of Djibouti by trying traditional dishes like skoudehkaris, sambusas, canjeero, and seafood specialties. Visit local restaurants and street food stalls to get a taste of the local cuisine.

Central Mosque: Visit Djibouti City's central mosque, a symbol of the city, and admire its architectural beauty. While non-Muslims are generally not allowed inside, you can appreciate the exterior and its cultural significance.

Haramous Beach: Spend time at Haramous Beach, a popular spot for swimming and relaxing by the Red Sea. Enjoy the sea breeze and beautiful views of the coastline.

Le Marché de Sel (Salt Market): Explore the local salt market, where you can witness the extraction and trading of salt harvested from Lake Assal, a unique and important industry in Djibouti.

Day Trip to Lake Assal: Take a day trip to Lake Assal, one of Djibouti's most iconic natural wonders. Visit the immense salt flats, float in the hypersaline lake, and appreciate the otherworldly landscapes.

French Cultural Center: Attend cultural events, exhibitions, or language courses at the French Cultural Center, which reflects the strong French influence in Djibouti.

Hiking in the Goda Mountains: Explore the Goda Mountains, located near Djibouti City, through hiking and trekking. The area offers stunning landscapes and wildlife.

Coffee and Tea Culture: Experience Djiboutian tea and coffee traditions. Enjoy a cup of sweet, spiced tea or strong Djiboutian coffee at local cafes and engage in conversations with locals.

Photograph Unique Landscapes: Djibouti City and its surroundings offer unique landscapes, including volcanic features, rugged mountains, and the Red Sea coastline. Capture the beauty of these distinct environments with your camera.

Cultural Interactions: Engage with local communities to learn about their customs, traditions, and daily life. Djibouti's diverse population and rich cultural heritage provide opportunities for meaningful cultural exchanges.

Dolphin Watching: Consider taking a boat tour to Ras Ali for dolphin watching, just a short drive from Djibouti City.

While Djibouti City may not have an extensive list of tourist attractions, it offers a blend of cultural experiences and natural beauty that provides a unique and authentic travel experience. Be sure to respect local customs and traditions during your visit and take time to connect with the friendly people of Djibouti.

nightlife in Djibouti City

Djibouti City is not known for its bustling nightlife scene compared to many other cities around the world. The nightlife in Djibouti City is relatively quiet and more conservative due to the predominantly Muslim population and local customs. However, there are some places where you can enjoy an evening out, socialize, and experience a taste of the city's nightlife:

Hotels and Restaurants: Many of the upscale hotels in Djibouti City, such as the Djibouti Palace Kempinski and the Sheraton Djibouti Hotel, have restaurants and lounges that offer evening entertainment, such as live music, cultural performances, and themed nights. These venues are among the best options for a relaxed evening.

Cafes and Tea Houses: Djiboutian culture places a strong emphasis on socializing in cafes and tea houses. You can enjoy a cup of tea or coffee, flavored with traditional spices, while chatting with locals. It's a low-key but enjoyable way to experience local life.

Shisha Bars: Shisha (hookah) bars are popular in Djibouti City, and they provide a relaxed setting for an evening of conversation and shisha. These are often frequented by both locals and expats.

Local Eateries: Some local eateries and restaurants remain open into the evening, serving traditional dishes. While they may not be explicitly nightlife spots, they offer a chance to enjoy local cuisine in a casual setting.

French Restaurants: Given Djibouti's historical ties with France, you can find French restaurants in the city. Some of them have a more relaxed and cozy ambiance for an evening meal.

Hotel Bars: Several hotels in Djibouti City have bars where you can enjoy a drink in a quiet and comfortable atmosphere.

It's important to note that the nightlife in Djibouti City is more subdued compared to Western cities, and entertainment options are limited. The city is generally more vibrant during the daytime, with markets and cafes being busy. As a visitor, it's advisable to be respectful of local customs and adhere to any regulations regarding alcohol and nighttime activities.

While Djibouti City may not have a lively nightlife scene, it offers unique cultural experiences and the opportunity to connect with the friendly local population. If you're looking for a more vibrant nightlife, you may consider exploring the nightlife options in larger cities or tourist destinations in other countries.

hotels in Djibouti City

Djibouti City offers a range of hotels that cater to various budgets and preferences. While the city's hotel scene may not be as extensive as in some other destinations, there are several options that provide comfortable accommodations and often beautiful views of the Red Sea. Here are some of the best hotels in Djibouti City:

Djibouti Palace Kempinski: This luxurious beachfront hotel is one of the most prestigious in the city. It offers elegant rooms, international dining options, a private beach, a spa, and beautiful sea views.

Sheraton Djibouti Hotel: Located on the shores of the Red Sea, this well-known hotel provides comfortable rooms, multiple restaurants, a swimming pool, and easy access to the beach.

Acacias Hotel: Acacias Hotel offers modern and comfortable accommodations, making it a popular choice for both business and leisure travelers. The hotel features a restaurant, fitness center, and conference facilities.

Hotel La Siesta: A more affordable option, Hotel La Siesta provides simple and clean rooms in the heart of Djibouti City. It's a budget-friendly choice with a convenient location.

Hotel Residence de l'Europe: This boutique hotel offers a tranquil atmosphere and personalized service. It's a suitable option for those looking for a peaceful stay in the city.

Hôtel Djibouti: Situated in the city center, Hôtel Djibouti is known for its convenient location, affordability, and comfortable accommodations.

Djibouti Arta Palace: Located in the nearby town of Arta, this hotel offers a peaceful retreat from the city and is known for its serene surroundings and beautiful views.

Hotel Les Acacias Djibouti: This hotel is a popular choice for travelers who seek a comfortable stay at a reasonable price. It features well-appointed rooms and an on-site restaurant.

Please note that the hotel scene in Djibouti City may have evolved since my last update in September 2021. It's advisable to check the latest information, reviews, and recommendations from travel websites or contact the hotels directly for up-to-date details on accommodations, facilities, and services. Djibouti City offers a range of hotel options to suit different preferences and budgets, and you can enjoy the city's unique coastal setting during your stay.

Moucha Island

Moucha Island is a small, picturesque island located in the Gulf of Tadjoura, just off the coast of Djibouti. It's known for its stunning beaches, clear waters, and coral reefs, making it a popular destination for those seeking relaxation and water-based activities. Here are some of the things you can see and do on Moucha Island:

Beaches: Moucha Island boasts pristine, white sandy beaches with crystal-clear waters. You can relax on the beach, swim in the sea, or soak up the sun. The peaceful atmosphere and breathtaking views make it an ideal spot for unwinding.

Snorkeling: The waters around Moucha Island are teeming with marine life and coral formations. Snorkeling is a must-do activity here, allowing you to explore the underwater world, spot colorful fish, and admire the coral reefs.

Diving: Scuba diving is a popular activity on Moucha Island. Several dive shops and operators offer dive trips to explore the underwater wonders, including coral gardens and the possibility of encountering sea turtles and other marine species.

Boat Tours: Take boat tours around Moucha Island to explore the coastline, visit hidden coves, and enjoy scenic views. Some tours may also offer the opportunity to spot dolphins in the surrounding waters.

Swimming and Water Sports: Besides snorkeling and diving, you can enjoy other water sports such as kayaking, paddleboarding, and swimming in the calm and clear sea.

Bird Watching: Moucha Island is a great place for birdwatching, with various bird species that inhabit or visit the island. Bring your binoculars to observe the birdlife.

Camping: Some visitors choose to camp on Moucha Island, enjoying a night under the stars in the tranquil environment. It's an excellent way to experience the island's natural beauty.

Local Cuisine: Local vendors may offer fresh seafood and local cuisine, allowing you to savor a delicious meal with the flavors of the sea.

Relaxation: With its serene atmosphere, Moucha Island is an ideal place to simply unwind, read a book, or enjoy a leisurely picnic on the beach.

Moucha Island is a hidden gem in Djibouti, known for its natural beauty and opportunities for water-based activities. It provides an escape from the hustle and bustle of Djibouti City and offers a peaceful and unspoiled coastal experience. Whether you're into snorkeling, diving, or just looking to relax, Moucha Island is a wonderful destination for a day trip or an overnight stay.

foods from Moucha Island

Moucha Island, being a small and remote island, doesn't have a bustling culinary scene, but it does offer some delightful and simple foods that are perfect for enjoying by the beach. Many of the dishes you'll find here are influenced by Djiboutian and East African cuisine. Here are some of the best foods you can savor on Moucha Island:

Seafood: Given the island's location in the Gulf of Tadjoura, fresh seafood is the highlight. You can enjoy grilled fish, prawns, lobster, and octopus, often seasoned with local spices. The simplicity of freshly caught seafood is a must-try.

Fresh Fruits: Moucha Island, like other parts of Djibouti, offers a variety of fresh fruits. Depending on the season, you can enjoy fruits such as mangoes, bananas, papayas, and citrus fruits.

Local Snacks: Local vendors may offer snacks such as sambusas, which are savory pastries filled with minced meat, vegetables, and spices. They make for a delicious and convenient beachside snack.

Grilled Meat: Some beachside eateries may offer grilled meat dishes, such as kebabs or skewers, which are seasoned and cooked over an open flame.

Traditional Djiboutian Tea: You can enjoy sweet and spiced Djiboutian tea, often flavored with cardamom and other spices, at local cafes and eateries. It's a refreshing beverage to accompany your meal or relax by the beach.

Fruit Juices: Local vendors may prepare fresh fruit juices, offering a cool and refreshing way to quench your thirst.

Picnics: Many visitors to Moucha Island choose to bring their own picnics, including sandwiches, fruits, and snacks, to enjoy a meal by the beach or during a day of exploration.

Please note that the dining options on Moucha Island are limited, and the emphasis is on simple, fresh, and local fare. The main attraction is the natural beauty of the island and the tranquility it offers. Be prepared to enjoy the relaxing atmosphere and the sound of the waves while savoring the flavors of Djibouti's coastal cuisine.

restaurants in Moucha Island

Moucha Island is a small and relatively remote island in Djibouti, known more for its natural beauty and outdoor activities than for its restaurant scene. While you won't find an extensive selection of restaurants on the island, there are a few places where you can enjoy a meal or a snack during your visit. These establishments are typically small and offer simple but delicious food, often focusing on seafood. Here are a couple of options to consider:

Local Beachside Cafes: Moucha Island has a few small local cafes and eateries right on the beach, where you can enjoy grilled seafood, traditional Djiboutian dishes, and refreshing beverages. These rustic, casual spots offer an authentic dining experience with a view of the sea.

Resort or Tour Operator Facilities: If you are staying at a resort or participating in a guided tour on the island, the resort or tour operator may provide dining options. Resorts often offer seafood and international dishes in a relaxed and tranquil setting.

Remember that dining options on Moucha Island are more about enjoying the natural beauty and outdoor activities than experiencing gourmet cuisine. The charm of the island lies in its unspoiled beaches, clear waters, and the opportunity to unwind in a serene environment. You can expect to enjoy fresh seafood, grilled dishes, and traditional Djiboutian flavors in a casual and laid-back atmosphere.

lesser known travel spots in Moucha Island

Moucha Island, with its pristine beaches and clear waters, is relatively small and tranquil, making it a destination focused on relaxation, water-based activities, and natural beauty. While it doesn't have a wide range of tourist attractions, there are a few lesser-known spots on the island that can add depth to your visit:

Baga Beach: While the main beaches on Moucha Island are well-known, Baga Beach, located on the western side of the island, is a quieter and less-visited spot. It offers tranquility and a peaceful atmosphere for sunbathing and swimming.

Lighthouse: The island's lighthouse is a lesser-visited attraction. You can explore the lighthouse and take in panoramic views of the island and the surrounding seas.

Bird Watching: Moucha Island is home to a variety of bird species, and birdwatching can be a rewarding activity. Bring your binoculars and observe the birdlife in the coastal and island habitats.

Trekking and Nature Walks: While the island is not large, there are opportunities for trekking and nature walks to explore its landscapes, from the sandy beaches to rocky coastlines. These activities allow you to connect with the island's natural beauty and coastal flora.

Camping: Some visitors opt to camp on the island, which provides a unique and immersive experience. Camping on the beach or in designated areas allows you to appreciate the tranquility of Moucha Island, especially at night when you can stargaze.

Underwater Photography: If you're a scuba diver or snorkeler, consider exploring the lesser-known coral formations and marine life for underwater photography. There are many colorful and unique marine species to capture.

Sunset Watching: While watching the sunset is a well-loved activity, the western side of the island, particularly around Baga Beach, offers a quieter and less crowded spot to enjoy the sunset in a serene setting.

Moucha Island's allure lies in its unspoiled beauty and serene atmosphere. While it may not have a long list of attractions, the island is a perfect destination for travelers seeking relaxation and outdoor activities, such as snorkeling, diving, and water sports. Exploring the less-visited areas of the island allows you to appreciate its natural charm and escape the crowds.

activities in Moucha Island

Moucha Island, with its pristine beaches and crystal-clear waters, is an ideal destination for relaxation and outdoor activities. While the island is relatively small, there are several activities you must experience during your visit to make the most of its natural beauty. Here are some of the activities to enjoy on Moucha Island:

Swimming: The clear and calm waters surrounding the island make it perfect for swimming. You can take a dip in the sea and enjoy the refreshing experience.

Snorkeling: The underwater world around Moucha Island is teeming with marine life and colorful coral reefs. Snorkeling is a popular activity, allowing you to explore the diverse aquatic environment.

Scuba Diving: If you're a certified diver, consider taking scuba diving excursions to explore deeper underwater landscapes and witness a wide range of marine species.

Beach Relaxation: Simply relax on the island's pristine sandy beaches, soak up the sun, and enjoy the tranquil ambiance. The beaches are excellent for sunbathing, reading, or having a picnic.

Water Sports: Depending on the local facilities, you can engage in water sports like kayaking, paddleboarding, and jet-skiing, providing an active way to enjoy the sea.

Beachcombing: Moucha Island's shores are ideal for beachcombing. You can search for seashells, coral fragments, and unique finds washed up by the tides.

Bird Watching: The island is home to various bird species, so consider bird watching to observe and identify the local avian life.

Picnics: Plan a beachside picnic with local snacks or your own packed meal. It's a great way to enjoy a leisurely lunch with a view.

Camping: If you're an outdoor enthusiast, camping on Moucha Island allows you to spend the night under the stars and fully experience the island's peaceful ambiance.

Sunset Watching: Moucha Island offers stunning sunsets, making it a fantastic place to watch the sun dip below the horizon and capture beautiful photographs.

Hiking and Nature Walks: While the island is not large, you can explore the coastal landscapes through hiking and nature walks. These activities allow you to connect with the natural beauty of the island.

Underwater Photography: If you're into photography, capture the vibrant marine life and coral formations with underwater photography. The island's waters offer excellent opportunities for stunning shots.

Moucha Island provides a tranquil and unspoiled environment, perfect for outdoor enthusiasts and those looking for relaxation by the beach. The variety of water activities, coupled with the island's natural beauty, make it an attractive destination for travelers seeking a laid-back and serene experience.

how is the nightlife in Moucha Island and what are the best nightlife spots

Moucha Island is primarily a destination for relaxation, water-based activities, and enjoying the natural beauty of its beaches and clear waters. Unlike larger cities and tourist hubs, Moucha Island does not have a vibrant nightlife scene. The island is known for its serene and tranquil atmosphere, making it an ideal place to unwind and escape the hustle and bustle of city life.

While there may be some options for evening entertainment and relaxation, the emphasis on Moucha Island is on enjoying the pristine beaches, clear seas, and outdoor activities during the day. Some ways to spend your evenings on the island include:

Beachside Strolls: Take a leisurely walk along the beach and enjoy the sound of the waves and the gentle sea breeze. Moucha Island is known for its beautiful sunsets, making it a romantic spot for evening walks.

Star Gazing: The lack of light pollution on the island offers excellent opportunities for stargazing. Lay back on the beach and admire the clear night sky.

Camping: If you're camping on the island, your evenings will be filled with campfires, storytelling, and the experience of sleeping under the stars.

Relaxing at Your Accommodation: Many visitors choose to relax at their resort or hotel during the evening hours. Some accommodations may offer entertainment or cultural activities.

Dining: Enjoy local seafood and cuisine at beachfront restaurants or your accommodation. The dining experience on Moucha Island is more about savoring delicious food in a peaceful setting rather than late-night revelry.

Local Cafes: Some local cafes or beachside vendors may offer beverages and snacks in the evening. It's an opportunity to interact with fellow travelers and enjoy the island's ambiance.

It's essential to set your expectations correctly when it comes to nightlife on Moucha Island. The emphasis here is on the island's natural beauty and the tranquility it offers, making it an ideal destination for those seeking a peaceful and laid-back retreat. If you're looking for vibrant nightlife, you may need to explore options in Djibouti City or other more urban areas in Djibouti.

hotels in Moucha Island

Moucha Island, located in Djibouti, offers a more limited selection of accommodations compared to some larger tourist destinations. It's known for its natural beauty and outdoor activities, making it an ideal destination for those who seek a serene and unspoiled environment. Here are a couple of places to consider for your stay on Moucha Island:

Moucha Island Beach Camp: Moucha Island Beach Camp is a popular choice for travelers seeking a laid-back and beachfront experience. It offers basic but comfortable beachfront huts, tents, and camping facilities. The camp provides an opportunity to stay close to the beach and enjoy a rustic island experience.

Resort and Diving Centers: Some of the water sports and diving operators on the island provide accommodations as well. These facilities are often more tailored to divers and water sports enthusiasts, offering simple yet convenient lodgings.

Please note that accommodations on Moucha Island tend to be more modest and cater to travelers who prioritize outdoor activities and natural beauty over luxury. It's advisable to book accommodations well in advance, especially during peak tourist seasons. Keep in mind that the charm of Moucha Island lies in its serene and unspoiled environment, making it a peaceful retreat for those looking to unwind by the sea.

Arta Plage

Arta Plage, located in the town of Arta in Djibouti, is a picturesque coastal area known for its natural beauty and tranquil atmosphere. While it may not have a wide range of tourist attractions, the area offers a unique setting for relaxation and appreciation of Djibouti's coastal landscape. Here's what you can see and do in Arta Plage:

Beaches: Arta Plage is primarily known for its beautiful sandy beaches. You can spend time on the beach, swim in the sea, and soak up the sun. The calm and clear waters make it a great spot for swimming.

Mousa Island: Mousa Island, also known as Maskali Island, is located just off the coast of Arta. It's a popular destination for boat trips, snorkeling, and diving, offering opportunities to explore the underwater world and vibrant marine life.

Boat Tours: You can take boat tours around the coastline to explore the scenic beauty of the Gulf of Tadjoura, including views of Mousa Island and the surrounding landscapes.

Bird Watching: Arta Plage and the nearby coastal areas are home to a variety of bird species. Birdwatching can be a rewarding activity for nature enthusiasts.

Relaxation: The tranquility of Arta Plage makes it an ideal spot for relaxation. You can unwind on the beach, enjoy a picnic, or read a book while listening to the waves.

Dining: Some local eateries may offer fresh seafood and local cuisine, allowing you to savor a delicious meal with the flavors of the sea.

Sunset Watching: The serene atmosphere of Arta Plage provides a perfect setting for watching the sunset. Enjoy the breathtaking views as the sun sets over the Gulf of Tadjoura.

Hiking and Nature Walks: The surrounding coastal and rocky landscapes are excellent for hiking and nature walks. Explore the natural beauty of the area and observe the coastal flora and fauna.

Arta Plage's allure lies in its unspoiled coastal beauty and tranquil ambiance. It's a destination for relaxation, coastal exploration, and appreciation of Djibouti's natural landscapes. Whether you're seeking a peaceful day at the beach, an outdoor adventure, or a scenic boat trip, Arta Plage offers a serene and unspoiled coastal experience.

foods from Arta Plage

Arta Plage, a coastal area in Djibouti, offers a range of delicious foods that showcase the country's culinary traditions, with a focus on fresh seafood. The local cuisine reflects a fusion of flavors from Africa and the Middle East. While you may not find as many dining options as in larger cities, here are some of the best foods to try in Arta Plage:

Fresh Seafood: Arta Plage is renowned for its fresh catch of the day, which often includes fish, prawns, lobster, and other seafood. Grilled fish and seafood dishes are popular and provide a taste of the sea's bounty.

Sambusas: Sambusas are savory pastries filled with minced meat, vegetables, and spices. They are a common snack or appetizer and offer a burst of flavors in each bite.

Canjeero: Canjeero is a type of Somali pancake, resembling a thin and spongy flatbread. It's often served with a variety of toppings, such as honey or spicy sauces.

Rice Dishes: Rice is a staple in Djiboutian cuisine. You can enjoy rice-based dishes, such as skoudehkaris (a rice and vegetable dish) and bariis iskukaris (spiced rice with meat or fish).

Local Spices and Seasonings: Djiboutian cuisine incorporates various spices, including cardamom, cinnamon, cumin, and coriander. These spices add depth and richness to the flavors of local dishes.

Fresh Fruits: Djibouti's climate allows for the cultivation of a variety of fruits, including mangoes, papayas, and bananas. These fruits are often served fresh and make for a refreshing dessert or snack.

Djiboutian Tea: Traditional Djiboutian tea is sweet and spiced, often flavored with cardamom and other spices. It's a popular beverage to complement your meal or simply enjoy as a refreshing drink.

Flatbreads: Various types of flatbreads, like injera, lahooh, and lahoh, are staples in Djiboutian cuisine and are often served alongside dishes.

While Arta Plage may not have a plethora of restaurants, you can savor these local flavors at beachside eateries and seafood shacks. The emphasis here is on enjoying the freshness of the sea and the simplicity of the cuisine. Be sure to try the local seafood dishes, as they are among the best culinary offerings in this coastal area.

restaurants in Arta Plage

Arta Plage, located in Djibouti, is a relatively small coastal area known for its natural beauty and tranquil atmosphere. While it may not have a wide range of dining options, you can find some local eateries and seafood shacks where you can enjoy delicious seafood dishes and traditional Djiboutian cuisine. Here are a couple of dining establishments to consider in Arta Plage:

Local Seafood Shacks: Some of the best dining experiences in Arta Plage can be found at the local seafood shacks and eateries situated along the coast. These establishments typically serve freshly caught seafood, including fish, prawns, and lobster, prepared in a simple yet flavorful manner. Grilled fish is a popular choice, and you can savor the taste of the sea while enjoying views of the beach.

Beachfront Cafes: Beachfront cafes and informal eateries in the area may offer a range of traditional Djiboutian dishes, including rice-based meals, sambusas (savory pastries), and spiced tea. These cafes provide a relaxed setting for enjoying a meal with a view of the sea.

Local Markets: While not traditional restaurants, local markets in the area may offer street food and snacks, providing an opportunity to taste some of the local flavors. You might find small stalls selling grilled meats, snacks, and fresh produce.

Please keep in mind that the dining scene in Arta Plage is more focused on simple and authentic flavors, with an emphasis on fresh seafood. Dining options are limited compared to larger cities, but the quality of the seafood and the coastal ambiance add to the charm of eating in this scenic coastal area.

lesser known travel spots in Arta Plage

Arta Plage, while known for its scenic coastal beauty, is a relatively small and tranquil area in Djibouti, and it doesn't have a wide range of tourist attractions or lesser-known travel spots. Nevertheless, if you're interested in exploring off the beaten path, here are a few suggestions to enhance your visit to the area:

Local Villages: Explore the nearby local villages to experience the daily life and culture of the region. Engaging with the local community can provide valuable insights into Djibouti's traditions and way of life.

Arta Mountains: The nearby Arta Mountains offer opportunities for hiking and trekking. The rocky landscapes and arid terrain provide a unique setting for outdoor exploration.

Bird Watching: The coastal and rocky areas around Arta Plage can be rewarding for birdwatching. Djibouti is home to various bird species, and you may spot interesting avian wildlife during your explorations.

Historical Sites: While Arta Plage itself may not have historical sites, you can inquire about the possibility of visiting nearby historical attractions, such as old forts, ruins, or cultural sites that hold significance in Djibouti's history.

Photography: The unique coastal landscapes and natural beauty of Arta Plage and its surroundings offer ample opportunities for photography. Capture the stunning seascapes, rock formations, and local scenes.

Cultural Experiences: Seek out cultural experiences by interacting with the local communities, participating in traditional activities, or learning about local customs and traditions.

Picnics and Beach Activities: While not exactly lesser-known, you can make the most of your visit by having a picnic on the beach, swimming, and enjoying the serene ambiance of the coastal area.

Arta Plage's charm lies in its unspoiled coastal beauty and tranquil atmosphere. While it may not have a plethora of tourist attractions, it offers a peaceful and unexplored experience for those who appreciate nature, culture, and outdoor activities.

activities in Arta Plage

Arta Plage, known for its scenic coastal beauty and tranquil atmosphere, offers a range of activities that allow you to appreciate the natural surroundings and local culture. While the area is relatively small and not heavily developed, there are several experiences you can enjoy during your visit:

Beach Relaxation: Spend time on the pristine sandy beaches of Arta Plage. Whether you're swimming in the clear waters, sunbathing, or simply strolling along the shoreline, the beach is perfect for relaxation.

Seafood Dining: Arta Plage is famous for its fresh seafood, and you must savor the catch of the day. Enjoy grilled fish, prawns, and lobster at local seafood shacks and eateries.

Bird Watching: The coastal area and nearby rocky landscapes are ideal for birdwatching. Bring binoculars and observe the diverse bird species in the region.

Boat Tours: Consider taking a boat tour to explore the Gulf of Tadjoura and the nearby Mousa Island (Maskali Island). These tours often include snorkeling opportunities and the chance to spot marine life.

Sunset Watching: The tranquil atmosphere of Arta Plage provides an excellent setting for watching the sunset. The breathtaking views of the sun setting over the Gulf of Tadjoura are a highlight.

Cultural Experiences: Interact with the local community to learn about Djibouti's culture and traditions. Visit local villages, try traditional foods, and immerse yourself in the local way of life.

Hiking and Nature Walks: The rocky landscapes and coastal areas surrounding Arta Plage are great for outdoor exploration. Hiking and nature walks allow you to connect with the natural beauty of the region.

Photography: The stunning coastal landscapes and unique natural features are perfect for photography. Capture the beauty of the sea, the rocky shores, and local scenes.

Local Markets: If there are local markets nearby, explore them to sample local snacks and purchase souvenirs. You might find fresh produce, crafts, and traditional goods.

Water Sports: Depending on local facilities, you can engage in water sports such as kayaking, paddleboarding, and jet-skiing, providing an active way to enjoy the sea.

Arta Plage offers a serene and unspoiled coastal experience, making it an attractive destination for travelers seeking relaxation and outdoor activities. Whether you're into beachside relaxation, water adventures, or cultural interactions, the area provides a peaceful and picturesque setting for a memorable visit.

nightlife in Arta Plage

Arta Plage is a relatively small and tranquil coastal area in Djibouti, known for its natural beauty and serene atmosphere. It doesn't have a vibrant nightlife scene like larger cities and tourist destinations. The emphasis in Arta Plage is on relaxation, coastal exploration, and appreciation of the peaceful environment.

While you won't find bustling nightlife spots, you can enjoy a quiet and serene evening by the beach or at your accommodation. Here are some ways to spend your evenings in Arta Plage:

Beachside Strolls: Take leisurely walks along the beach and enjoy the calming sound of the waves and the sea breeze. Arta Plage is known for its beautiful sunsets, making it a romantic spot for evening walks.

Star Gazing: The lack of light pollution on the coast of Arta Plage offers excellent opportunities for stargazing. Lay back on the beach and admire the clear night sky.

Dining: Many of the local seafood shacks and eateries may offer evening meals with fresh catch and traditional Djiboutian cuisine. Enjoy a seafood dinner with the soothing sounds of the sea as your backdrop.

Relaxing at Your Accommodation: If you're staying at a resort or hotel, enjoy the facilities and accommodations. Some resorts may offer entertainment or cultural activities in the evening.

Local Cafes: Some local cafes or beachside vendors may offer beverages and snacks in the evening. It's an opportunity to interact with fellow travelers and enjoy the tranquil ambiance.

Arta Plage is a destination where the focus is on the natural beauty and the peaceful atmosphere. It's not known for vibrant nightlife, and the charm of the area is the opportunity to relax by the beach and immerse yourself in the serene coastal environment. If you're looking for a more lively nightlife scene, you may need to explore options in Djibouti City or other urban areas in Djibouti.

hotels in Arta Plage

Arta Plage, located in Djibouti, is known for its serene coastal beauty, but it is a relatively small area and doesn't have a wide selection of hotels and resorts compared to larger tourist destinations. Accommodations in Arta Plage are typically more modest and cater to travelers seeking a tranquil beachside experience. Here are a couple of places you can consider for your stay in Arta Plage:

Seafront Bungalows and Cabins: Some establishments in Arta Plage offer seafront bungalows or cabins that allow you to stay close to the beach. These accommodations often provide a rustic yet comfortable beach experience.

Resort Accommodations: Some resorts and diving centers in the area may offer lodging options. These facilities are often more tailored to divers and water sports enthusiasts. They provide simple but convenient accommodations with beach access.

Please note that accommodations in Arta Plage tend to be more basic and focused on providing a beachfront experience, rather than luxury. While the area is not known for a wide range of hotel options, it is prized for its natural beauty, clear waters, and the opportunity to relax in a tranquil coastal setting. Be sure to book your accommodations in advance, especially during peak tourist seasons.

beaches in Djibouti

Djibouti, with its stunning coastline along the Red Sea and the Gulf of Aden, is home to several beautiful beaches. These beaches offer clear waters, vibrant marine life, and opportunities for relaxation and water-based activities. Some of the best beaches in Djibouti include:

Doraleh Beach: Located near the Port of Doraleh, this beach offers a scenic view of the Red Sea. It's known for its clear waters and is a popular spot for swimming and picnicking.

Khor Ambado Beach: Situated on the outskirts of Djibouti City, Khor Ambado Beach is known for its sandy shores and calm waters. It's an excellent place for swimming and taking in the views of the Gulf of Tadjoura.

Arta Plage: Located in the town of Arta, this picturesque beach offers a tranquil atmosphere and is surrounded by natural beauty. It's ideal for relaxation, beachcombing, and snorkeling.

Moucha Island: Accessible via a short boat ride, Moucha Island is known for its pristine beaches, clear waters, and excellent opportunities for snorkeling, diving, and water sports.

Tadjoura Beach: The town of Tadjoura is home to a charming beach with golden sand and calm waters. It's an excellent spot for swimming, sunbathing, and enjoying a peaceful coastal atmosphere.

Obock Beach: Obock, located in the northern part of Djibouti, offers scenic beaches along the Gulf of Tadjoura. The beaches are tranquil and provide an escape from the hustle and bustle.

Ras Siyyan Peninsula: This remote and undeveloped area offers rugged coastal beauty and stunning landscapes. It's a fantastic destination for hiking and exploration.

Ghoubbet al-Kharab: Located near the Devil's Island, Ghoubbet al-Kharab is known for its unique natural features and is a popular spot for diving and exploration.

Djibouti's beaches are known for their natural beauty, making them ideal for relaxation and outdoor activities. Whether you're into swimming, snorkeling, or simply unwinding by the sea, the country's beaches offer a diverse range of coastal experiences.

. what other spots are there along the Djibouti coastline

Djibouti's coastline along the Red Sea and the Gulf of Aden is dotted with a variety of scenic and unique spots, from picturesque beaches to rugged landscapes and vibrant marine environments. Here are some other notable spots along the Djibouti coastline:

Tadjoura: This historic town along the Gulf of Tadjoura is known for its picturesque beach, as well as its well-preserved colonial architecture. It offers opportunities for swimming, relaxation, and cultural exploration.

Ras Siyyan Peninsula: Located at the southern entrance of the Red Sea, this remote and rugged peninsula is known for its unique landscapes, rocky cliffs, and pristine beaches. It's a great spot for hiking and nature enthusiasts.

Ghoubbet al-Kharab: Also known as the Gulf of Ghoubbet or the Gulf of Tadjoura, this unique and highly saline body of water is known for its otherworldly landscapes. The Devil's Island, located in this area, is a popular destination for divers and adventurers.

Gulf of Aden: This vital waterway is known for its historical and strategic importance. While not typically a destination for leisure, it offers impressive maritime views and opportunities for observing ships from various nations passing through.

Moucha Island: Accessible via a short boat ride from Djibouti City, Moucha Island is known for its pristine beaches and clear waters. It's a popular destination for snorkeling, diving, and water sports.

Obock: This town in the northern part of Djibouti offers beautiful beaches along the Gulf of Tadjoura. It's known for its tranquility and remote location, making it an escape from the busier areas of the country.

Lake Assal: While not directly on the coastline, Lake Assal is a unique destination. It's the lowest point in Africa and the second saltiest lake in the world. It offers opportunities for photography and experiencing the natural wonder of Djibouti.

Doraleh Port: This major seaport is located near Doraleh Beach and is an interesting place to observe shipping operations and the busy commercial activity along the coast.

Khor Ambado: Located near Djibouti City, Khor Ambado is a popular spot for beachgoers, with its calm waters and sandy shores. It's a great place for swimming and picnicking.

The Djibouti coastline offers a diverse range of landscapes and experiences, from pristine beaches to unique geological formations. Whether you're interested in relaxation, water sports, exploration, or cultural experiences, Djibouti's coastal areas have something to offer for travelers seeking diverse coastal experiences.

shopping experiences in Djibouti

Djibouti, a small country in the Horn of Africa, offers a range of shopping experiences for visitors, from traditional markets to modern shopping centers. While the shopping scene in Djibouti may not be as extensive as in larger cities, there are still interesting and unique places to explore. Here are some of the best shopping experiences in Djibouti:

Central Market (Marché Central): This bustling market in Djibouti City is a great place to immerse yourself in the local culture and shop for traditional goods. You'll find an array of items, including clothing, fabrics, jewelry, spices, and souvenirs. Be prepared to haggle, as bargaining is common in this market.

Héron Souvenir Market: Located near the Kempinski Hotel, this market specializes in souvenirs and handicrafts. You can find items like traditional Djiboutian clothing, woven baskets, and local art, making it an excellent place to pick up mementos of your trip.

Djibouti's Shopping Centers: The country has modern shopping centers like Etablissement Bilal, which features a range of shops, including international and local brands. These centers are air-conditioned and provide a more contemporary shopping experience.

Local Artisan Workshops: Explore local workshops and stores that sell artisanal goods, such as textiles, pottery, and traditional jewelry. These unique pieces can be a special addition to your collection.

Attarine Market: Located in the capital, Attarine Market is a vibrant and bustling place where you can find an assortment of goods, from fresh produce to electronics and clothing. It's an excellent opportunity to experience everyday life in Djibouti.

International Food and Grocery Stores: If you're interested in exploring international flavors or purchasing goods from your home country, you can visit stores like Casino Supermarché or City Market, which offer imported products.

Duty-Free Shopping: Djibouti-Ambouli International Airport has duty-free shops where you can buy items like perfumes, electronics, and luxury goods at more affordable prices.

Traditional Clothing Stores: Seek out traditional clothing shops to purchase Djiboutian attire. You can find items such as dira dresses and macawiis for a unique and cultural fashion experience.

Keep in mind that the shopping experience in Djibouti is different from what you might find in larger cities, and it's advisable to have cash on hand, as credit card acceptance may be limited. Exploring the local markets and stores can be a fun and authentic way to connect with the culture and find unique items to take home as souvenirs.

historical sites visit in Djibouti

Djibouti, located at the crossroads of the Red Sea and the Indian Ocean, has a rich history that spans thousands of years. The country's strategic location has made it a cultural and historical melting pot. Here are some historical sites you can visit in Djibouti to explore its rich heritage:

Tadjoura: This historic town, one of the oldest in Djibouti, boasts well-preserved colonial architecture, including old stone buildings and houses. The town's charm lies in its ancient streets and architecture, giving you a glimpse into Djibouti's past.

Balbala Village: Balbala is known for its traditional Afar huts, which are made of natural materials. The village provides insight into the traditional way of life of the Afar people, who are one of the ethnic groups in Djibouti.

Arta Old Town: The town of Arta features traditional houses and structures, showcasing the traditional Afar architecture. It's a place to observe the historical roots of Djibouti's population.

The Maskali Island Tombs: Located on Maskali Island in the Gulf of Tadjoura, these ancient tombs are believed to be around 2,000 years old. They provide a glimpse into the early history of the region.

Mogadishu Street in Djibouti City: Mogadishu Street in Djibouti City is known for its historical houses, which feature a blend of African and Arabic architectural influences. It's a charming area to explore and capture the historical atmosphere.

The Plateau du Serpent: This plateau, located near the village of Dikhil, features ancient petroglyphs that are estimated to be thousands of years old. The rock engravings depict various animals and scenes of daily life from the region's early inhabitants.

Ancient Harar Dhow Harbor: This historical harbor, located in the town of Obock, was once a thriving trading port during the 19th century. It offers insights into the region's maritime history and the exchange of goods along the Red Sea.

Le Château d'Eau (Water Tower): Built in the early 20th century during the colonial period, this water tower is a historical landmark and a symbol of Djibouti's history. It's a unique architectural structure to visit in the heart of Djibouti City.

Djibouti Palace Kempinski: While not a historical site in the traditional sense, this luxury hotel is housed in a historic building, the former residence of the French Governor of Djibouti. It's a blend of colonial and Moorish architecture.

Ethnographic Museum of Djibouti: Located in Djibouti City, this museum showcases artifacts, tools, and objects that offer insights into the cultural history and traditions of Djibouti's various ethnic groups.

Visiting these historical sites allows you to delve into Djibouti's past and appreciate the rich tapestry of cultures and histories that have shaped the country. It's a unique opportunity to connect with Djibouti's heritage and learn about its historical significance.

Conclusion

Djibouti, a small yet diverse nation nestled in the Horn of Africa, offers a unique blend of natural beauty, cultural richness, and historical significance. As we conclude this travel guide to Djibouti, we hope you've been inspired to explore this hidden gem, often overshadowed by its larger neighbors. Djibouti has a lot to offer to adventurous travelers, from its pristine beaches along the Red Sea to the captivating landscapes of its desert and mountains.

You can experience the mesmerizing landscapes of Lake Assal, Ardoukoba Volcano, and Moucha Island. Dive into the cultural heritage of the country by visiting historical sites and exploring traditional villages, providing a deeper understanding of Djibouti's history and people.

Sample the flavors of Djibouti through its cuisine, savoring fresh seafood and local dishes that reflect a blend of African and Middle Eastern influences. Engage with the friendly locals and immerse yourself in their customs, making your journey a truly enriching experience.

While Djibouti may not have the extensive tourist infrastructure of some destinations, its unspoiled beauty and tranquil ambiance are part of its unique charm. From the bustling markets to the relaxed beaches, this country offers an authentic and peaceful escape for those who appreciate natural beauty and a glimpse into a different world.

As you plan your trip to Djibouti, take into account its climate, culture, and customs, and remember to respect the environment and local traditions. Whether you're an intrepid explorer seeking new horizons, a history enthusiast delving into ancient cultures, or simply a traveler in search of a serene coastal escape, Djibouti awaits you with open arms and the promise of unforgettable memories. So, pack your bags and embark on a journey to discover the hidden treasures of Djibouti. Bon voyage!

Description:

"Explore Djibouti: A Traveler's Guide to the Horn of Africa" is your passport to discovering one of the world's best-kept secrets. Nestled along the Red Sea and the Gulf of Aden, Djibouti is a small, uncharted paradise brimming with captivating landscapes, cultural treasures, and experiences waiting to be uncovered.

This comprehensive travel guide takes you on a virtual journey through Djibouti's hidden gems, from the pristine beaches of Lake Assal to the dramatic landscapes of Ardoukoba Volcano. Whether you're an intrepid explorer, a history enthusiast, or simply a traveler in search of tranquil coastal beauty, this guide offers valuable insights to make the most of your Djibouti adventure.

Inside, you'll find:

In-depth explorations of Djibouti's natural wonders, including its unique geological formations, tranquil islands, and wildlife-rich seas.

A tour of Djibouti's historical sites, where ancient traditions and rich heritage come to life.

A culinary adventure through Djibouti's diverse cuisine, from fresh seafood delicacies to vibrant spices.

Tips and recommendations for engaging with the warm-hearted locals, participating in cultural traditions, and understanding the customs of this unique nation.

Djibouti may not be as traveled as its neighbors, but this guide will help you navigate the unspoiled beauty, history, and culture that await you. Whether you're planning a journey to Djibouti or simply want to immerse yourself in its allure from afar, "Explore Djibouti" is your key to unlocking the treasures of the Horn of Africa. Embark on this adventure and let Djibouti's hidden wonders captivate your imagination.

Made in the USA
Coppell, TX
27 October 2024

39254477R00031